Lost Little Angel

Lost Little Angel

written by M. M. Ragz

illustrated by Jane Manning

Simon & Schuster Books
for Young Readers

SIMON & SCHUSTER BOOKS FOR YOUNG READERS
An imprint of Simon & Schuster Children's Publishing Division
1230 Avenue of the Americas, New York, New York 10020

Book design by Lily Malcom
The text of this book is set in Hiroshige.
The illustrations are rendered in watercolor.
Printed in Hong Kong
First Edition
10 9 8 7 6 5 4 3 2 1
Library of Congress Cataloging-in-Publication Data
Ragz, M. M.
Lost Little Angel / by Margaret M. Ragz.
p.   cm.
Summary: A young angel who gets lost in heaven reminds Saint Sebastian,
Saint Bridget, and the other saints of the joy that heaven is all about.
ISBN 0-689-81067-9
[1. Angels—Fiction. 2. Heaven—Fiction.] I. Title.
PZ7.R12717Lo 1999
[E]—dc20   96-44989
CIP   AC

For Nica and all angel-children
— M. M. R.

For Billy Lee
— J. M.

Once, long ago, a small angel-child named Nicholas lived in Heaven, Level One. He had lots of angel friends to play with, but his best friend in the whole of heaven was Comet, his dog. Together they tumbled through fields of golden grass, gathered starfish from the shores of the Endless Sea, and chased fireflies in the moonlight.

"Don't wander too far," the Guardian Angels told the children each morning. "And whatever you do, don't go beyond the Heavenly Hedge. You'll get lost for sure."

But Nicholas loved adventure, and when Comet chased a butterfly through a small hole in the Heavenly Hedge, Nicholas followed right behind.

The butterfly zigged, and Comet zigged. The butterfly zagged, and Comet zagged. After a while all this zigging and zagging left Nicholas quite tired—and quite lost.

He turned around and around, hoping to find the way back. Suddenly they were riding up a long golden staircase.

When they reached the top, all Nicholas could see were hurrying, scurrying feet and swirling, twirling robes. "Where in Heaven are we?" he asked.

He sat for a while. He was sure someone would stop to help him. But no one paid any attention . . . until a very tall angel tripped over Comet and came clattering down in a heap.

"A child? *And* a dog?" the angel bellowed in a voice that sounded like the wind on a stormy day. "Impossible! There are no children on this level of Heaven. And we certainly don't allow dogs. You'll have to leave."

The angel with him frowned and nodded.

"Okay," Nicholas said. "How?"

The angels looked confused. "I'm not sure," the crotchety angel finally said. "No one has ever left before. This, my dear child, is Level Nine of Heaven. It takes a long time to get promoted this high. You must be here by mistake. Come with us. Someone in the Hallowed Halls will know what to do." And off they marched—so fast that Nicholas had to run to keep up.

As they waited in a long, long line, Nicholas tugged at the robe of the big angel. "Excuse me, sir," he said. "Who are all these angels?"

The big angel looked down at him. "They're all very important. This is Saint Bridget," he said, introducing the angel who had come with them. "And that's Saint Leo, and there's Saint Cecilia talking to Saint Felicity, and Saint Bernard—"

"But who are *you?*" Nicholas interrupted, because he knew he'd never keep all those names in his head.

The angel cleared his throat and pulled himself up even taller. "I've been here the longest. I am Saint Sebastian. Who are you?"

"Just Nicholas," Nicholas answered.

"Well, Just Nicholas. You've picked a very bad time to get lost here. Especially since—"

But Nicholas couldn't hear another word. All of a sudden the air around them filled with a horrible noise—*clank! clunk! bingle! bang!*—like someone banging on giant pots with wooden spoons.

"What is *that?*" Nicholas yelled, covering his ears. Comet howled.

Suddenly all the banging and the clanging stopped.

"You mustn't shout, Just Nicholas," Saint Sebastian said, acting as if he had heard nothing.

The line inched forward. When the *rattle, jangle, thud* started again, Saint Bridget explained to Nicholas that their bells were broken. "I'm sure they'll be fixed soon," she said. "Especially with Saint Sebastian in charge."

When it was finally their turn, Saint Sebastian explained the problem of the lost little angel and his dog to the Ruling Council of Angels.

The council members looked first at Nicholas, then at Comet, and started talking all at once. Since no one had ever gotten lost before, they didn't know what to do. In the end it was decided that Nicholas would have to remain on Level Nine until Saint Sebastian could find the time to find an answer.

As they left the Hallowed Halls, Saint Sebastian said, "Try not to get in trouble, Just Nicholas. We have no time for a child, especially one with a dog. As soon as I figure out what to do with you, I'll let you know." And he swished his robes and strode away with Saint Bridget right behind.

"I guess they don't like us," Nicholas said, hugging Comet. For the first time in his whole angel life, big tears rolled down his cheeks.

He felt a hand on his shoulder, and when he looked up, there stood Saint Bridget holding a star pop for him and a moon bone for Comet. "Why don't you two come with me, Just Nicholas. I could use some help in my garden," she said, wiping his tears with the hem of her robe.

Nicholas and Comet stayed close to Saint Bridget as she wove in and out of angel traffic. "Why is everyone in such a rush?" Nicholas asked.

"Everyone has chores," she said. "When you get to Level Nine, you have a lot of responsibilities."

As they hurried on, every now and then the clunking and the twanging of the broken bells clattered through the air. "No wonder everyone is so grumpy," Nicholas thought. "I would be too if I had to listen to *that* all the time."

When they arrived at Saint Bridget's garden, Nicholas saw the saddest-looking crop of rainbows he had ever seen. "I don't know what's happened," she said. "My rainbows are all droopy."

As the clunky bells filled the air again, Nicholas said, "Maybe they can't grow because of the noise." But Saint Bridget didn't hear.

Nicholas worked in the garden for a while, but he got bored. When Saint Bridget went to get some raindrops for her garden, he and Comet wandered off looking for adventure.

Nicholas had never seen so much hustle and bustle. Angels who weren't rushing to get somewhere were busy working. Some were painting the sunrise while some dusted away cloud-webs. Others were buffing the morning stars, and still others practiced shooting stars. There were angels polishing sunbeams, stitching long comet tails, assembling snowflakes, and waxing the moon.

Nicholas asked a few if they wanted to play, but those who even bothered to answer said, "Not now" or "Too busy" or "No time."

In the distance Nicholas saw a giant bank of clouds that looked like great drifts of snow.

"What fun!" he said, jumping into the clouds and rolling around. "Woof," Comet said, hopping after him. Nicholas picked up a handful of cloud, patted it into a ball, and flung it as hard as he could at Comet. But he missed and *whap!* hit a passing angel right in the head, almost knocking his halo off. Another angel started to giggle.

"Oh, you think that's funny, do you?" the angel with the crooked halo asked as he clomped over to the cloud bank. He scooped up an armful of cloud and chucked it at the giggling angel, but she ducked and *smack!* the cloud hit someone else.

It didn't take long before a whole host of angels were in the middle of a cloudball fight. A few of the most serious saints jumped into the cloud bank and started rolling balls for a cloudman.

Saint Bridget came hurrying over, watering can in hand, and seeing the fun everyone else was having, kicked off her sandals, fell into the cloud bank, and made a cloud angel.

They were all having a wonderful time laughing and playing, until Saint Sebastian appeared before them. "What *are* you doing?" he asked, his voice more rumbly than usual.

The laughing stopped.

"Who fixed the bells?" he added. When the angels looked puzzled, he said, "You were all making so much noise, you didn't even notice. Be quiet and listen!"

They listened. But all that filled the air was the usual *clang, bang, clunk,* and *clatter* of the broken bells. Saint Sebastian looked sad.

Nicholas wondered if the angels were going to cry. Then he had an idea. He whispered in Saint Bridget's ear. Very slowly she picked up a handful of cloud and tossed it toward Saint Sebastian. It arched through his halo and landed with a *plop* right on top of his head.

Everyone froze. Saint Sebastian's face turned redder and redder. He took a breath as deep as the north wind. Just as he was about to speak, a piece of the cloudball slid down and hung, like an icicle, off his nose.

Saint Bridget giggled. Saint Leo chuckled. Saint Felicity laughed. And the fun began again.

All at once, through the laughter, they heard the bells. No *clanks* or *clunks*. No *bingles* or *bangs*. But golden jingles and silver chimes rang through the skies.

Everyone stopped to listen. The bells stopped. Saint Bridget giggled again, and a soft tinkling filled the air.

Saint Sebastian scratched his head. "Well, I'll be," he said, and started to smile. His smile was followed by his laugh, a great booming laugh that rolled up from his toes. And as he laughed, they heard the echo of the grandest bell of all.

Saint Sebastian gathered Nicholas up in his huge arms. "Well, Just Nicholas. It took a small lost boy—and his dog—to remind us what Heaven is all about." He looked out at the crowds of angels that had assembled around them. "And from this day forward, all angels should take the time to have some fun . . . and to laugh every day."

Saint Sebastian asked Nicholas to stay with them on Level Nine. Nicholas said, "Thank you, sir. But I miss my friends. I wish you could help me find my way home."

Saint Sebastian sighed and said, "I'm sorry. I just don't know how—"

Suddenly Saint Bridget ran up, all excited. "You should see my rainbows," she said, and laughed. "They're *huge*!" Sure enough, rainbows filled the heavens all around them.

"There's your way home, Just Nicholas," Saint Sebastian said. "But you must promise to visit now and then. Just in case we forget and get too busy again. And someday, when you become Saint Nicholas, perhaps you will give your gifts of joy and laughter to the whole world."

As all the saints gathered to wave good-bye,
Nicholas slid down a rainbow—with Comet
right behind. All the way down to Level One,
Nicholas could hear the glorious sound of the
golden bells.